D1528560

A Celebration of the Civil Rights Movement ™

MARTIN LUTHER KING JR. AND THE SPEECH THAT INSPIRED THE WORLD

Erin Staley

ROSEN PUBLISHING®

New York

Published in 2015 by The Rosen Publishing Group, Inc.
29 East 21st Street, New York, NY 10010

Library of Congress Cataloging-in-Publication Data

Staley, Erin.
Martin Luther King Jr. and the speech that inspired the world/Erin
Staley.—First edition.
    pages cm.—(A celebration of the civil rights movement)
Includes bibliographical references and index.
ISBN 978-1-4777-7745-9 (library bound)
1. King, Martin Luther, Jr., 1929–1968—Juvenile literature. 2. African
Americans—Biography—Juvenile literature. 3. Civil rights workers—
United States—Biography—Juvenile literature. 4. Baptists—United
States—Clergy—Biography—Juvenile literature. 5. African Americans—
Civil rights—History—20th century—Juvenile literature. 6. Civil rights
movements—United States—History—20th century—Juvenile literature.
7. United States—Race relations—Juvenile literature. I. Title.
E185.97.K5S69 2014
323.092—dc23
[B]

2013049331

Manufactured in the United States of America

CONTENTS

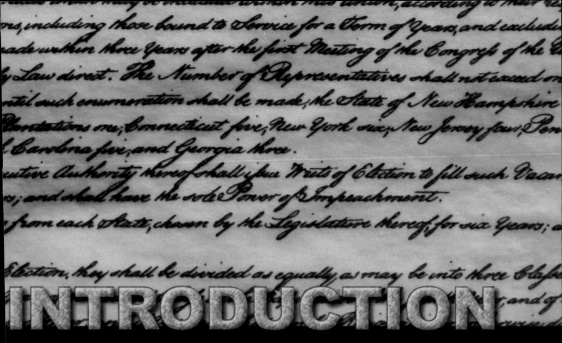

I t is the Declaration of Independence (1776) that proclaims, "We hold these truths to be self-evident, that all men are created equal." Equal. A five-letter word that is easy to write but difficult to implement in a country that was built on the backs of slaves.

During the Civil War, President Abraham Lincoln's (1809–1865) Emancipation Proclamation (1863) freed the slaves. However, the effects of slavery continued for over one hundred years, namely in the segregated South. African Americans were not considered to be first-class citizens and were told where to live, where to worship, where to sit, and where their children could attend school. They were not allowed to enjoy the same freedoms as their white countrymen.

Year after year, African Americans were subjected to racial humiliation. But there was hope. Leaders within the black community rose up. They were tired of seeing friends, family, and

Martin Luther King Jr., pictured here at a 1964 press conference, was a leading force behind the nonviolent pursuit of civil rights in the United States.

neighbors subjected to social, political, and professional walls of discrimination. Fed up with the degradation, they set forth to claim what was rightfully theirs: "Equality for all." As a result, these leaders established the most influential social movement of the twentieth century in the United States—the civil rights movement (1945–1968).

This movement began with the idea that men, women, and children could bring about long-lasting social change using a nonviolent approach. Civil rights leaders called upon their communities to take action despite social pressure, crooked law enforcement, stifling legislation, and physical threats. These courageous leaders organized nonviolent protests, marches, sit-ins, and boycotts to make their voices heard and their actions seen. Their passion united the black community and stirred the hearts of sympathetic whites to join their efforts. Throughout the civil rights movement, people of all races stood shoulder to shoulder to change the perspective of a nation.

While there are a number of noteworthy civil rights leaders—both in history books and behind the scenes—we are going to look at the work of one man whose name is synonymous with the American civil rights movement: Dr. Martin Luther King Jr.

Husband, father, minister, activist, and Nobel Peace Prize recipient, Dr. King was one of the most influential civil rights leaders in the world. From his first speech as a teenager to the last speech he delivered before his assassination, Dr. King championed for a united society in which every person could enjoy his or her freedom. For decades, he put his beliefs—and his safety—on the line for the rights granted us by America's most important documents.

The following pages will reveal bits of Dr. King's life and several key events that led to that memorable day in 1963 when he stepped to the podium and delivered his famous speech, "I Have A Dream." We will also discover how his speech inspired change in social behavior as well as in federal legislation. You will see that Dr. King's immortal speech not only transformed a nation but encouraged the world to look beyond the color of one's skin and toward the dream of "equality for all."

Chapter 1

THE AWAKENING OF A MIRACLE

Michael King, who would later become the celebrated American civil rights leader Martin Luther King Jr., was born on January 15, 1929, in Atlanta, Georgia. He was the second child of the Reverend and Mrs. Michael King Sr. Young Michael and his family lived in the home of his maternal grandparents, Reverend and Mrs. Adam Daniel Williams. Although they shared a comfortable lifestyle in the Sweet Auburn neighborhood—home to many prominent African Americans—Michael and his family were surrounded by the ugliness of racial segregation.

Every week young Michael and his family attended Ebenezer Baptist Church, where his grandfather was the pastor. When Reverend Williams died in 1931, Michael's father took

King's father, Reverend Martin Luther King Sr., also participated in nonviolent protests. He is pictured here *(second man on the left)* reading the Bible on a segregated bus in 1957.

JIM CROW LAWS STEAL FREEDOM

After the Confederacy surrendered in the Civil War, the Reconstruction period (1865–1877) was established to heal the war-torn nation. Some states developed Black Codes to control the migration of free African Americans. Nevertheless, Southern legislators went a step further. They quickly passed laws that appeared to be fair to the black community: the right to marry, own property, and enter into contracts. Yet their Black Codes offered only second-class citizenship and stripped away the rights granted by the Thirteenth, Fourteenth, and Fifteenth Amendments to the U.S. Constitution. Because of the deceptive nature of these laws, the Black Codes were given the nickname "Jim Crow laws." Jim Crow was a popular song-and-dance character played by a white actor wearing blackface. The entertainer mocked African Americans for the amusement of white audiences. Crow's racial disguise mimicked the deceptive nature of the Black Codes.

Jim Crow laws enforced segregation in public places. Signs told whites where they could go and "coloreds" where they could not. African Americans were not allowed to drink from the same water fountains or use the same restrooms as whites. They were made to sit in the back of public buses and could not exercise their right to vote. They were even buried in separate cemeteries. African Americans faced discrimination in housing, banking, and employment situations. Consequently, humiliation, bitterness, and fear prevailed in the hearts of many within the black community.

his place at the pulpit. The son of Georgia sharecroppers, King Sr. became a leader in state and national Baptist and civil rights groups. He preached against poverty, discrimination, and segregation. On a trip to the Holy Land and then Germany, he had been inspired by the life of German monk Martin Luther (1483–1546). Luther had greatly influenced a religious movement to reform sixteenth-century Roman Catholicism. As a result, Protestantism was established. King Sr. honored the reformist by naming himself and his five-year-old son Martin Luther King.

THE JOURNEY BEGINS

Martin Luther King Jr. was like most boys. He loved football and baseball, worked as a paperboy, and dreamed of becoming a fireman. In his junior year of high school, he demonstrated natural speaking abilities by winning a 1944 oratory contest titled "The Negro and the Constitution."

Martin left Booker T. Washington High School because of his early admittance into Atlanta's Morehouse College. Although it was the alma mater of his father and maternal grandfather, Martin was reluctant at first to follow in their footsteps. He was more interested in law or medicine. But Morehouse's president, Dr. Benjamin E. Mays, became his mentor. He was an advocate for racial equality and encouraged his young apprentice to consider Christianity as a catalyst for social change. Martin read the works of great philosophers, including *Civil Disobedience* by Henry David Thoreau (1817–1862), and was hooked by their values. His first steps as a political activist included a 1946 letter to the editor of the city's largest newspaper, the *Atlanta Constitution*. It stated:

> We want and are entitled to the basic rights and opportunities of American citizens: The right to earn a living at work for which we are fitted by training and ability; equal opportunities in education, health, recreation, and similar public services; the right to vote; equality before the law; some of the same courtesy and good manners that we ourselves bring to all human relations.

KING'S PHILOSOPHY TAKES SHAPE

In February 1948, nineteen-year-old King Jr. was ordained assistant pastor at Ebenezer Baptist Church. In June, he graduated from Morehouse College with a bachelor of arts degree in sociology. As September approached, he traveled to Pennsylvania to become one of six African Americans enrolled at Crozer Theological Seminary. Here,

Crozer's Dean Charles Batten described King as "one of the best men in our entire student body." He noted King was "held universally in high regard by faculty, staff, and students."

King was drawn to philosophers such as Aristotle, Plato, Locke, Hegel, and Rousseau. He was also intrigued by the work of the theologian Reinhold Niebuhr (1892–1971). He admired Niebuhr's Christian take on the social challenges of the modern day. He was also introduced to the nonviolent teachings of India's Mohandas Gandhi (1869–1948). With Gandhi's leadership, millions of Indians used civil disobedience to protest British rule. King learned that the hatred of one's enemies is immoral and only continues the vicious cycle of vengeance. In Time-Life's *I Have a Dream: The Story of Martin Luther King in Text and Pictures,* King acknowledged the influence of Gandhi's work on his own way of thinking. He was quoted as saying, "The spirit of passive resistance came to me from the Bible and the teaching of Jesus. The techniques of execution came from Gandhi."

After graduating at the top of his class with a bachelor of divinity (1951) degree, King enrolled in Boston University's School of Theology doctoral program. While in Massachusetts, King met Coretta Scott (1927–2006), an Alabama native and New England Conservatory of Music student. The two were married by King Sr. in 1953 and made a home for themselves in Montgomery, Alabama. In October 1954, King was appointed pastor of

King is greeted by his wife after leaving a Montgomery courthouse in 1956. Although he was found guilty of conspiracy to boycott city buses, his $500 fine was suspended.

Dexter Avenue Baptist Church. Still a graduate student, he was elected president of his predominantly white senior class and went on to earn his Ph.D. in systematic theology in 1955.

REFUSING A SEAT IN ORDER TO TAKE A STAND

In November 1955, the Interstate Commerce Commission legally banned segregation on interstate travel buses and in bus stations. Nevertheless, segregation continued. African Americans challenged this practice with sit-ins and boycotts, but it wasn't until a department store seamstress refused to give up her seat that real change occurred.

Rosa Parks's act of bravery, along with the leadership of those in the community, triggered one of the nation's most crucial and successful protests. *The Autobiography of Martin Luther King Jr.* notes Dr. King's outlook on the December 5 boycott:

Fortunately, a bus stop was just five feet from our house. We [King and his wife] could observe the

Booked, fingerprinted, and briefly incarcerated, Rosa Parks (1913–2005) was arrested for her quiet act of defiance. She became known as the "Mother of the Civil Rights Movement."

opening stages from our front window. And so we waited through an interminable half hour. I was in the kitchen drinking my coffee when I heard Coretta cry, "Martin, Martin, come quickly!" I put down my cup and ran toward the living room. As I approached the front window, Coretta pointed joyfully to a slowly moving bus: "Darling, it's empty!" I could hardly believe what I saw. I knew that the South Jackson line, which ran past our house, carried more Negro passengers than any other line in Montgomery, and that this first bus was usually filled with domestic workers going to their jobs. Would all of the other buses follow the pattern that had been set by the first?

Dr. King jumped in his car to find out. Only a few passengers were on the other buses. It was a vision. Boycott leaders met on Monday afternoon and established the Montgomery Improvement Association (MIA). The newly formed group needed an energetic president who could peacefully rally the black community. Dr. King was that leader. He addressed the crowd with powerful words, as noted in *A Call to Conscience: The Landmark Speeches of Dr. Martin Luther King Jr.*:

My friends, there comes a time when people get tired of being trampled over by the iron feet of oppression. There comes a time, my friends, when people get tired of being plunged across the abyss of humiliation, where they experience the bleakness of nagging despair. There comes a time when people get tired of being pushed out of the glittering sunlight of life's July,

ROSA PARKS SETS A MOVEMENT INTO ACTION

Montgomery's public bus system represented the extreme restrictions of segregation in the South. *The Papers of Martin Luther King Jr.: Volume III: Birth of a New Age, December 1955–December 1956* points out Dr. King's observances:

> He [a visitor to Montgomery before the boycott] would have frequently noticed Negro passengers getting on the front door and paying their fares, and then being forced to get off and go to the back doors to board the bus, and often after paying that fare he would have noticed that before the Negro passenger could get to the back door, the bus rode off with his fare in the box. But even more that visitor would have noticed Negro passengers standing over empty seats.

This racial injustice inspired Edgar Daniel "E. D." Nixon. He was the civil rights activist who thought an arrest offered the perfect opportunity to challenge Montgomery's bus policy. He presented the idea to Parks, a member of the National Association for the Advancement of Colored People (NAACP). She agreed and refused to give up her seat to a white passenger on December 1, 1955. Parks was arrested and jailed. Immediately, a one-day boycott was scheduled for December 5, the day of her trial. Black passengers were encouraged to stay home or take alternate means of transportation. Approximately thirty-five thousand notices went up all over town, and black ministers spread the word through sermons. Over forty thousand people joined the movement, and their efforts forever changed American history.

and left standing amid the piercing chill of an alpine November. There comes a time.

Dr. King called for unity despite fear and intimidation. He declared that people had the right to protest in an American democracy. He challenged them to keep God first and practice Christian love and justice.

WHEN PUSH COMES TO SHOVE

Without hesitation, MIA members unanimously voted to carry on with the boycott. Black commuters traveled by foot, carpool, or black-operated cabs. Dr. King even drove people to and from work. The public transit system and downtown businesses lost thousands of dollars without African American passengers to ride the buses or shop in the stores. Still segregation continued, and so did the boycott. White segregationists struck back. They stopped black cabs that had been undercharging black passengers. They cancelled insurance policies for vehicles that carried black commuters. Drivers, including Dr. King himself, were arrested for violating minor—and often imaginary—traffic laws. When the schemes proved ineffective in putting a stop to the boycott, segregationists resorted to violence.

On a January evening in 1956, Dr. King attended a mass meeting while his wife was home with their seven-and-a-half-week-old daughter, Yolanda Denise. Around 9:15 PM, Coretta heard a thud outside. She hurried to the back room to check on the baby. A bomb exploded. Glass went flying. Dr. King rushed home to find both his wife and his daughter uninjured. He then calmly addressed hundreds of infuriated neighbors waiting outside. Dr. King proclaimed that he did not advocate for violence but for love. He was adamant that the civil rights work would not stop. God was with them. The crowd rallied behind him, and law enforcement pledged to protect the King family.

Efforts continued to desegregate Montgomery's public transit system. A black legal team took the issue to the U.S. District Court. In June 1956, the court declared racial segregation laws to be unconstitutional. The city of Montgomery appealed the decision, but the U.S. Supreme Court sustained the ruling. The 381-day Montgomery bus boycott officially ended on December 20, 1956, thanks to the bravery of a unified community.

Chapter 2

THE CONSCIENCE OF A NATION

With the success of the Montgomery bus boycott, Martin Luther King Jr. was catapulted onto the national stage of the civil rights movement. Teaming up with other activists, he founded the Atlanta-based Southern Christian Leadership Conference (SCLC) in January 1957. Its purpose was to support local civil rights campaigns and pursue full equality with nonviolent resistance according to spiritual principles. "Not one hair of one head of one person should be harmed" was the motto. Dr. King became the SCLC's first president, a position he held until his death in 1968.

"THE CLOCK OF DESTINY"

On May 17, Dr. King spoke at the Prayer Pilgrimage for Freedom in Washington, D.C. It was his first public address. Approximately twenty thousand people attended as King and other leaders nudged the federal government to enforce *Brown v. Board of Education of Topeka, Kansas* (1954). In *Brown*, the U.S. Supreme Court determined "segregated schools are

On May 17, 1957, as racial tension escalated across the country, King enthusiastically implored the Prayer Pilgrimage for Freedom crowd to support national civil rights reform.

not equal and cannot be made equal, and hence they are deprived of the equal protection of the laws." Unfortunately, many Southern schools dragged their feet when it came to integrating black students into their all-white schools.

The three-hour Prayer Pilgrimage for Freedom program was filled with music, testimonies, and addresses. The last presenter was Dr. King. His speech, "Give Us the Ballot, We Will Transform the South," expounded on integration and addressed the issue of voting. Jim Crow laws had restricted African Americans, especially when it came to casting their votes. Literacy tests were required in many Southern states,

SODA, SEGREGATION, AND SELF-DETERMINATION

It was 1955 when fifteen-year-old Lolita Kelsey Adair traveled from her Pennsylvania home to her maternal grandmother's home in North Carolina. She reunited with her cousin, and the girls spent their time laughing and sharing stories. One morning, their grandmother asked them to pick up a prescription at the uptown pharmacy. They happily set out for the mile-long walk.

Hot and thirsty, Lolita plopped down at the pharmacy's lunch counter and offered her cousin a soda. With eyes wide as saucers, her cousin whispered, "You can't sit there." Lolita looked around. Everything seemed normal.

"You're going to be in trouble," her cousin hissed before walking to the back to pick up the prescription. This time, Lolita noticed customers scowling at her. A waitress scurried past her to take food orders from new arrivals and refused to serve her. Reluctantly, Lolita left the pharmacy and headed home. Horrified by the news, their grandmother stopped her rocker and headed inside. From the front porch, Lolita could hear her grandmother on the phone, apologizing to the listener and explaining that her "granddaughter was from the North and didn't know any better."

Despite the confidence Lolita's grandmother had displayed within the family, she "knew her place" within the segregated community. That was the day Lolita vowed to never cower in the face of inequality. She dedicated her life's work to equality for all as a real estate agent in northeast Ohio and as the first black female broker in Summit County. Through the years, she served on a number of real

> estate boards and fair housing committees. Today, she celebrates the fact that men, women, and children of all races can live in their dream home, have a say in their community, and enjoy a refreshing soda at any lunch counter across the country.

but a large number of African Americans couldn't pass the tests and were therefore unable to vote.

On the steps of the Lincoln Memorial, Dr. King appealed to the conscience of the nation. He humbly challenged the government to take decisive action and remove the voting barriers. According to *"Making a Way Out of No Way": Martin Luther King's Sermonic Proverbial Rhetoric*, Dr. King defined the situation as a moral issue that will decide our nation's destiny "in the ideological struggle with communism. The hour is late. The clock of destiny is ticking out."

Dr. King claimed both political parties betrayed black people with undemocratic practices and prejudicial hypocrisy. He implored his countrymen to commit to racial justice. He stressed the urgency of leadership within the black community and encouraged agape love. He exhorted them to pray for their enemies or else history would repeat itself. But he was not just idealistic in his vision. He knew it would take sleepless nights, suffering, and maybe even death. According to *"Making a Way Out of No Way,"* Dr. King stated, "But if physical death is the price that some must pay to free their children from a permanent life of psychological death, then nothing can be more Christian."

LITTLE ROCK PREPARES FOR SCHOOL INTEGRATION

Time was needed to enforce the new integration laws, especially in the Jim Crow South. Segregation had been a way of life, and in the case of the Little Rock Nine, it took a group of brave teenagers to claim what was rightfully theirs: a quality education. In 1954, federal law instructed school boards to integrate and provide the same quality education for all students. This meant no more hand-me-down textbooks and supplies, no more broken-down heaters and plumbing, and no more second-rate education. The School Board of Little Rock, Arkansas, responded to the federal decree. At the time, the state was considered to be moderate. It had already integrated African Americans in several state universities. Therefore, integration wouldn't be such a drastic move—or so they thought.

The School Board of Little Rock created a three-part desegregation plan. It would begin in 1957. However, the U.S. Supreme Court added a 1955 order: desegregation ought to be done "with all deliberate speed." Again, the school board responded favorably. School officials began a rigorous interview process to determine which African American students would be enrolling in Central High School, the largest school in Little Rock. Elizabeth Eckford, Minnijean Brown, Ernest Green, Thelma Mothershed, Melba Pattillo, Gloria Ray, Terrance Roberts, Jefferson Thomas, and Carlotta Wells were selected. They were scheduled to start on the first day of school, September 3, 1957. The plan was to meet in the morning and walk into school as a group, escorted by two white and two black ministers.

Governor Orval Faubus was in office at the time. Although considered a moderate Democrat, he was facing a gubernatorial primary election. He had the moderate vote but needed to appeal to extremists in his party. To do this, he called for 250 National Guardsmen to arrive at the school in early September. He claimed in a televised speech that the measures were merely preventative. The community believed Faubus's efforts were to protect the nine students who were eagerly anticipating their new educational adventure.

A BRAVE TEENAGER FACES A HATE-FILLED MOB

On the morning of the fourth, fifteen-year-old Elizabeth Eckford headed for Central High School. But she had not received the message to meet the other eight students as her family did not own a telephone. When she arrived at Central High School that morning, a hate-filled mob of students, parents, and community members greeted her. Daisy Bates, a prominent black leader, recounted Elizabeth's words in *The Long Shadow of Little Rock: A Memoir*:

> The crowd moved in closer and then began to follow me, calling me names. I still wasn't afraid. Just a little bit nervous. Then my knees started to shake all of a sudden and I wondered whether I could make it to the center entrance a block away. It was

The school year is tainted by racism as Arkansas National Guardsmen deny Elizabeth Eckford entrance into Little Rock Central High School.

the longest block I ever walked in my whole life.

The guards refused to let Elizabeth pass. She did, however, notice another guard farther down who was admitting white students. She walked up to him, but he raised his bayonet. The crowd became increasingly aggressive. Some participants called for her lynching. Now she was frightened. Again, Bates quoted Elizabeth in *The Long Shadow of Little Rock:* "I looked into the face of an old woman and it seemed a kind face, but when I looked at her again, she spat on me." Elizabeth found a nearby bench where a white man sat beside her. Bates recalled Elizabeth's words: "He raised my chin and said, 'Don't let them see you cry.'" Eckford eventually made it home as the other eight Little Rock students faced the same threats and were denied entry into Central High School.

"BLOOD WILL RUN IN THE STREETS"

Americans were appalled by the news. According to *The Long Shadow*

Arkansas's thirty-sixth governor, Orval E. Faubus, discusses integration of Little Rock schools at a press conference. He eventually softened his pro-segregationist views later in his political career.

of Little Rock, Governor Faubus explained his actions on television. He had heard that white supremacists from all over Arkansas would be congregating at the school, and he wanted to avoid a disaster. But in the same address, Faubus revealed all by saying "blood will run in the streets" if the students entered Central High School. The result was a string of back-and-forth legalities between Faubus, President Dwight D. Eisenhower (1890–1969), the court system, and the Little Rock School Board.

Despite his defiance of federal law, Governor Faubus kept the National Guardsmen in place. Dr. King wrote a telegram warning President Eisenhower that inaction could set integration back significantly. Following a September 14 meeting with the president, Faubus agreed to give his full cooperation. Again the troops remained. Meanwhile, NAACP lawyers filed a petition to remove the National Guard. On September 20, it was granted, and Faubus was obligated to let integration continue. He then surprised the nation by pulling the National Guard out entirely on September 23. This left the students—and a handful of police escorts—to face one thousand angry protesters alone. The Nine slipped through a side door, but riots broke out when the mob discovered that they had made it into the school. The Nine narrowly escaped.

Although Eisenhower issued an emergency proclamation ordering the mob to disband, they stayed on school grounds. In response, he sent 1,200 federal troops from the army's 101st Airborne Division to defend the Nine. It was the first time since Reconstruction that a president sent federal troops to protect the constitutional rights of African Americans. Dr. King responded with gratitude. He praised President

Eisenhower for his decision and mentioned that the majority of Southerners stood behind him in his efforts to restore law and order. Eventually, the Little Rock Nine were able to walk into Central High School. Although the taunts and death threats continued, the Nine courageously attended classes for the rest of the year. Ernest Green became the first to graduate, and Dr. King attended his ceremony. In 1958, the Little Rock Nine were given the NAACP's highest honor, the Spingarn Medal, for their determination and historical contribution.

THE FREEDOM RIDERS

Not only was segregation an issue in schools, it was also alive and well on the highways and byways of the South. Twice the U.S. Supreme Court declared segregation to be a violation of Interstate Commerce laws—once in 1946 and again in 1960. To make sure the law stuck the second time, a group called the Congress of Racial Equality (CORE) organized Freedom Riders. The 1961 movement was made up of black and white civil rights demonstrators who were ready to "climb aboard" interstate buses and test the new legislation. The law gave them the freedom to sit anywhere on the bus. But CORE leaders and Dr. King had their concerns. Rumors were flying: the Ku Klux Klan (KKK) claimed the Freedom Riders would never make it through Alabama.

ROLLING INTO ANNISTON

On May 14, Mother's Day, a Freedom Riders bus was making its way toward Anniston, Alabama. The town had a 30 percent African American population and a well-established

NAACP branch. But it also had a thriving KKK chapter. A riot-ous mob of Klansmen greeted the riders in Anniston. Armed with clubs, chains, and metal pipes, they shouted obscenities, smashed windows, and slashed tires. No arrests were made. Police simply escorted the mangled Greyhound bus out of the parking lot to another location. Again, the mob assault continued. A flaming wad of rags was thrown into the bus. It exploded, filling the bus with smoke. The riders, choking on fumes, got out just in time. Fists were raised and blood was spewed. Onlookers gathered in the distance, and twelve-year-old Janie Miller offered water to the victims despite jeering Klansmen. Warning shots from highway patrolmen

Freedom Riders look on as their Greyhound bus burns. Although a devastating incident, it led to one of the most pivotal events in the ongoing battle for racial equality.

caused the mob to disperse before the lynching could begin. To compound matters, obtaining medical attention was difficult. Reluctant ambulance drivers, unwilling police escorts, an understaffed hospital, and threats of arson made it almost impossible. With the help of civil rights leader Reverend Fred Shuttlesworth (1922–2011), the Freedom Riders were able to flee Anniston.

About an hour later, the Trailways bus arrived in Anniston. Its journey had been plagued from the moment it left the terminal. Klansmen had boarded and were taunting the other riders. At a bus stop in Alabama, the driver exited and the beatings began. Despite their efforts to remain calm, two black students were punched and kicked. Two white activists were beaten for trying to help. All four men were tossed in the back of the bus. A police officer returned with the bus driver, but no arrests were made. The ride continued into Birmingham, but this was the city of the notorious police commissioner Eugene "Bull" Connor (1897–1973). He had ties to the KKK and was ferocious about white supremacy and state's rights. Connor had prepared his own welcome for the Freedom Riders: a fifteen-minute "free-for-all." Klansmen pushed, shoved, punched, and kicked the Riders. They used baseball bats, lead pipes, and anything else they could get their hands on. When word spread that police were on their way, the mob disappeared. No one was arrested for the assault, and most of the Freedom Riders were evacuated to New Orleans. The rides continued that summer, with four hundred riding in the name of freedom. By the fall of 1961, the Interstate Commerce Commission banned segregation from interstate travel and in all transportation facilities.

Chapter 3

"BLACK IS BEAUTIFUL!"

The year 1963 marked the one hundredth anniversary of the Emancipation Proclamation. And yet, racial tensions agitated certain pockets of the country. Birmingham, Alabama, earned the nickname "Bombingham" for the eighteen bombings that took place there between 1957 and 1963. Stabbings, chain whippings, and street draggings terrorized the black community, especially when the guilty parties were not brought to justice. In response, Dr. King and the SCLC teamed up with Reverend Fred Shuttlesworth and the Alabama Christian Movement for Human Rights to create the Birmingham Campaign.

THE BIRMINGHAM CAMPAIGN

A three-member city commission had long governed the city of Birmingham, but in 1963, the city held a mayoral election. The Commissioner of Public Safety, Bull Connor, ran against former Alabama Lieutenant Governor Albert Boutwell. The result was a tie, but Boutwell took the victory in the run-off election. Civil rights leaders took the opportunity to fight for segregation in public places besides schools. They hosted marches as well as sit-ins at lunch counters, libraries, and all-white churches. They even encouraged a boycott of downtown stores during Easter weekend—one of the biggest moneymaking shopping times of the year. Civil rights leaders believed the campaign would bring about a peaceful desegregation compromise with the business community.

Soon, a state circuit court injunction was issued against demonstrations of any kind. Campaign leaders were forced to decide if their actions were worth imprisonment. To add to the dilemma, financial resources were low. Leaders could no longer afford bail money for jailed protestors. This was especially true for Dr. King, who was a key fund-raiser. *Character Is Destiny: Inspiring Stories Every Young Person Should Know and Every Adult Should Remember* notes Dr. King's opinion: "We cannot in all good conscience obey such an injunction which is an unjust, undemocratic, and unconstitutional misuse of the legal process." On April 12, 1963, Good Friday, Dr. King and SCLC associate Ralph Abernathy (1926–1990) defied the anti-protest injunction. They led a demonstration and were arrested.

Dr. King was kept in solitary confinement and was denied the right to call his wife, who was in Atlanta recovering from the birth of their fourth child. But during his imprisonment, he continued to protest. He took on white Birmingham clergy who criticized his civil disobedience methodology. In the margins of the *Birmingham News*, the very paper that printed the criticism, Dr. King defended his actions. He incorporated concepts from the Bible, the U.S. Constitution, and other texts to write his famed "Letter from Birmingham Jail." Eventually, he was able to call home, thanks to his wife's initiative. She had contacted President John F. Kennedy's

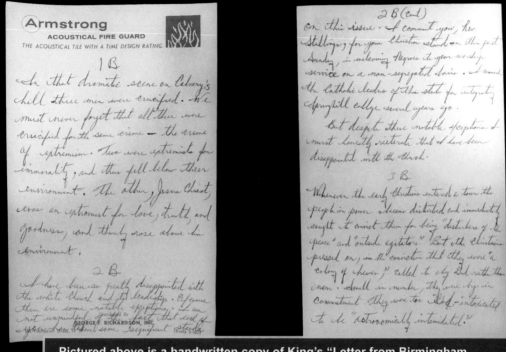

Pictured above is a handwritten copy of King's "Letter from Birmingham Jail." His words were so powerful that they swayed public opinion regarding nonviolent acts of civil disobedience.

(1917–1963) administration, making it possible for her husband and Abernathy to be released on April 20, 1963.

Meanwhile, social unrest continued. Demonstrators were arrested and given five-day jail sentences with $50 fines. To make matters worse, city commissioners refused to leave office. They did not recognize the authority of the newly elected mayor and his council members. Each party claimed power, but on April 23, the incoming officials were declared Birmingham's legal government. The city was in a tailspin, but nothing could have prepared it for what lie ahead.

TAKING THEIR PLACE IN THE CIVIL RIGHTS MOVEMENT

From the beginning of the civil rights movement, men and women had risked their lives for equality. But it wasn't until Reverend James Bevel, a SCLC leader and King adviser, proposed the Children's Crusade that the fight against segregation reached a new level. Bevel called for high school and college-age freedom fighters to participate in local demonstrations. Civil rights leaders debated this tactic, but in the end, the young people were ready to take their place in the civil rights movement.

On May 2, more than one thousand black students headed for the 16th Street Baptist Church. Younger sisters and brothers came along, too. With walking shoes on their feet and protest signs in their hands, the young people gathered for the 10-mile (16-kilometer) walk to Birmingham's downtown. Arrests were made by the hundreds. Students were hauled off in school buses and paddy wagons. But this didn't stop others from doing it all over again the following day. Again, arrests were made. Only this time, Connor directed police and firefighters to break up the demonstrations with high-pressure fire hoses. The children were doused, police officers clubbed them, and police dogs attacked. Many were injured, including Shuttlesworth, who had to be hospitalized.

Images of the incident were splashed across the front page of national newspapers. The American people were horrified. But despite the circumstances, the young freedom fighters kept their spirits up. They sang about freedom while sitting in overcrowded jails and fairground detainment areas. The Birmingham Children's Crusade showed the world that impassioned people—no matter what their age—can take a stand in the name of justice.

Although young demonstrators endured high-pressure fire hoses and police dogs in Birmingham, their courage brought about lasting changes to the country's civil rights reform.

A COMPROMISE IS REACHED

Boycott efforts were working. White businesses were losing money—lots of money. But it wasn't enough to convince business council members to negotiate. Attorney General Robert Kennedy (1925–1968) stepped in to help with negotiations. Although civil rights leaders disagreed to suspend mass demonstrations, Dr. King was in favor of peace. On May 10, the Birmingham Truce Agreement took shape. Schools, stores, and restaurants would be desegregated; employment opportunities would be upgraded; and jailed protesters would be released. To oversee the progress of the agreement, a biracial committee was assigned. The Birmingham Campaign appeared to be a success, and to make the victory even sweeter, Commissioner Connor was fired.

THE BIRMINGHAM SUMMER HEATS UP

Not everyone was rejoicing over the changes. Birmingham segregationists set off a bomb at the Gaston Motel where Dr. King was staying. He was unharmed, but three thousand federal troops arrived in Birmingham to prevent rioting. And this was just the start. For the rest of the summer, there were approximately one thousand demonstrations in more than two hundred cities across the United States. African Americans in the North had realized they were not spared from discrimination. They were denied housing opportunities and job advancement, and these were just as threatening

In February 1963, King gives a press conference outside of the Gaston Motel in Birmingham. His speechwriter, Clarence B. Jones *(left)*, looks on as King discusses a limited desegregation plan.

as the atrocities occurring to their sisters and brothers in the South. According to Debra Bell of USNews.com, black Congressman Charles C. Diggs Jr. from Michigan warned the government:

> If rational counsel is to prevail among the mass of Negroes, then Congress will have to give the moderates, such as myself, necessary weapons—and that means the whole civil-rights package. If the Negroes don't get their demands, they will turn to other leadership that will produce an even greater crisis than this one.

But some African Americans were no longer inclined to let the federal government right the wrong.

GEORGE WALLACE'S SCHOOLHOUSE STAND

Meanwhile in Alabama, Governor George C. Wallace (1919–1998) was making headlines. He refused to integrate Alabama's education system, and he put himself in the way of progress, literally. Wallace had studied at the University of Alabama and served in the air force during World War II before rising through the political ranks. In 1958, he ran for governor as a Democrat but lost to Alabama's attorney general, John Patterson. Patterson—endorsed by the KKK—claimed the reason behind his win was Wallace's soft approach to the race issue. Wallace agreed and was more determined than ever to win the next election. He hired a KKK speechwriter. "Segregation now! Segregation tomorrow! Segregation forever!" became

BLACK POWER IGNITES CHANGE

The term "Black Power" had been used since the 1950s, but Stokely Carmichael (1941–1998), the head of the Student Nonviolent Coordinating Committee (SNCC), was credited for popularizing it at a 1966 March Against Fear rally. Influenced by Malcolm X (1925–1965), a Muslim minister and human rights activist, Carmichael rejected integration in favor of racial self-determination. He believed that whites had control, and a purely black society would need to rise up to fight for equal employment opportunities, mortgage rates, and safer neighborhoods. SNCC and CORE chapters rejected their white membership in favor of separationist ideals.

Despite Dr. King's denouncement of Black Power, the movement made a lasting impression on the black community. Blacks advocated for themselves and reclaimed their African heritage. "Black is beautiful!" became a slogan as African American students adorned their bodies and homes with African-inspired styles. No more whitening creams and hair straighteners.The term "Negro"—which had been used since the days of slavery—was replaced with the term "black."

The Black Power movement had never been officially structured, and there were various groups within the movement. In late 1966, the Black Panther Party for Self-Defense was formed to protect Oakland, California, neighborhoods against police brutality. Black Panthers soon spread across the United States and so did their militant efforts. Among Black Power followers, there was division on the approach to the white community. One faction thought the other too soft, while the other faction thought them too eager to pull the trigger. As the years progressed, the Black Power movement scattered. But the effect was long lasting, as African Americans were both proud and empowered.

his campaign slogan. When addressing the matter of school integration, Wallace told voters he would stand in the schoolhouse door before abiding by an illegal federal court order. Victory was his in the next election.

Wallace's conviction was put to the test when two black students, Vivian Malone and James A. Hood, attempted to enroll at the University of Alabama in Tuscaloosa. On the morning of June 11, 1963, Wallace defiantly took his place in front of the schoolhouse door. Federal authorities asked him to step aside, but he refused. He announced the legal basis for his presence and challenged the presence of the federal government. A few hours later, officials returned with Alabama National Guard troops, who had been called into federal service by President Kennedy. Rather than provoke a violent reaction, Wallace stepped down. A few hundred onlookers watched as U.S. Marshals escorted the two students into the building. They enrolled without incident, but Wallace's role in the day's events would forever shadow his legacy.

Chapter 4

AT THE TABLE OF BROTHERHOOD

If 1963 proved anything, it was that activists could draw national attention. Tensions were at an all-time high, and the world was watching. Civil rights leaders knew there was no time like the present to do something big, and they turned to history for inspiration.

FROM THE PAGES OF HISTORY

In 1941, A. Philip Randolph (1889–1979), president of the Brotherhood of Sleeping Car Porters, proposed a March on Washington after African Americans suffered from job discrimination. President Franklin D. Roosevelt (1882–1975) had shown little interest in tackling the problem. Randolph and fellow leaders forged ahead and called for fifty thousand attendees to join them. Their actions forced Roosevelt to issue Order 8802 forbidding discrimination by industry contractors and establishing the Fair Employment Practices Committee. As a result, the march was canceled.

In the wake of a tumultuous 1963, Randolph knew a march would be the ideal way to put the civil rights movement on the

LIFE

Another Sacrifice by Fire
**FLAMES OF FURY
IN VIETNAM**

HOLLYWOOD'S GREAT ENIGMA,
BURT LANCASTER

In Color:
**SPECTACLE
of the
MARCH**

NEW
YORK
EXTRA
SECTION

THE LEADERS:
RANDOLPH
AND RUSTIN

SEPTEMBER 6 · 1963 · 25¢

Life magazine features A. Phillip Randolph and Bayard Rustin in the September 6, 1963, issue. Both were activists and organizers for the March on Washington for Jobs and Freedom.

international stage. It was called the March on Washington for Jobs and Freedom. Rudolph chaired the event and black activist Bayard Rustin (1912–1987) organized it. Although it was designed to be a peaceful rally to end segregation and create equal job opportunities, the Kennedy administration was nervous. It didn't want the march to incite chaos and therefore requested that it be cancelled. Civil rights leaders adamantly refused. Too much was at stake. In turn, the Kennedy administration called on its resources. Federal Bureau of Investigation (FBI) and Secret Service agents would be on-site to mingle in the crowd and monitor the event from observation points. The police department would be prepared for looting and bank robberies. Area officers would undergo riot training, and local judges would be stationed in courtrooms. Jails and hospitals would make room for troublesome or injured protesters. Even the canine division would be ready, but because of the fiasco with the Children's Crusade, they would be kept in kennels. The military was slotted to help with an armed task force and helicopters. Government offices were to close with federal employees staying home. The sale of alcohol was banned for twenty-four hours. If an aggressive protester took control of the sound system during the speeches, an official would pull the cut-off switch and a recording of Mahalia Jackson's "He's Got the Whole World in His Hands" would play.

In addition, Rustin worked with the Kennedy administration to make sure that the march was peaceful. The Lincoln Memorial, the very monument that honored the president who had issued the Emancipation Proclamation, was chosen for its significance and its central location. Plus, the day's program was predetermined. Dr. King and other leaders, both black and white, would lead the march from the Washington

Monument to the Lincoln Memorial. The night before the event, August 27, each speaker turned in an advanced copy of his speech for the press. However, Dr. King arrived too late. He quickly wrote his address and after a few hours of sleep, prepared for the day that would embody the spirit of the civil rights movement.

More than two hundred thousand people from every corner of the United States made their way to Washington, D.C. Black, white, old, young—they lined up on either side of the Reflecting Pool, along the National Mall and toward the Washington Monument. Although temperatures were rising, spectators laughed, sang, embraced, and cheered. Entertainers such as Josephine Baker, Bob Dylan, and Joan Baez made appearances, lifting the crowds' spirits and evoking a sense of national pride. President Kennedy, who did not attend, joined millions of Americans who tuned in on their television sets. One by one, civil rights leaders addressed the crowd. Then it was time for the last speech of the day. All eyes were on Dr. King as he stepped up to the podium.

With the skill of a master orator, Dr. King emphasized the greatness of this highly anticipated event and its chosen location. What had been a beacon of hope for African Americans—the

Emancipation Proclamation—had become ineffective, causing his people to remain as outcasts in their own country. They were denied "certain unalienable Rights" as promised in the Declaration of Independence: "Life, Liberty and the

King delivers his "I Have A Dream" speech in front of a passionate March on Washington for Jobs and Freedom crowd on the Mall in Washington, D.C.

pursuit of Happiness." Now they were fighting back. The nation could no longer ignore the urgency of the times. Dr. King called for democracy, racial justice, and brotherhood. He also addressed the African American community, reminding them that in the midst of this awakening, they must not turn to hatred and bitterness. Peace should rule, accompanied by discipline and dignity. The black man ought to trust the white man, he emphasized, noting their futures and freedoms were intertwined.

Despite his meaningful words, the crowd began to wither under the hot afternoon sun. Mahalia Jackson called out to him, saying, "Tell 'em about the dream, Martin." Dr. King then went off-script. With a thundering voice, he declared the following, as noted on Archives.gov:

> Though we face the difficulties of today and tomorrow, I still have a dream. It is a dream deeply rooted in the American dream. I have a dream that one day this nation will rise up, live out the true meaning of its creed...I have a dream that one day on the red hills of Georgia, sons of former slaves and the sons of former slave-owners will be able to sit down together at the table of brotherhood.

The crowd roared, calling out to him, "Dream on!" Invigorated, Dr. King then spoke of the distress in Southern states and the joining of hands of black and white children. He spoke of his own four children and his hope that they would be recognized for their character and not their skin color. He spoke of the opportunity to live and worship, work and pray one with another. Finally, he quoted "My Country 'Tis of Thee," a well-known American patriotic song. His voice became more assertive as he challenged the nation to "let freedom ring." Dr. King continued, according to Archives.gov:

> When we let it [freedom] ring from every city and every hamlet, from every state and every city, we will be able to speed up that day when all of God's children, black men and white men, Jews and Gentiles, Protestants and Catholics, will be able to join hands and sing in the words of the old Negro spiritual, "Free at last, Free at last, Great God a-mighty, We are free at last."

A thundering applause erupted. History had been written. As the civil rights leaders made their way to the White House for a preplanned post-event meeting with President Kennedy, reporters were feverishly drafting media reports to be broadcast nationwide. "I have a dream" was immortalized as the catchphrase of the civil rights movement. In fact, the entire March on Washington was regarded as the pivotal event in the movement. Its effects were felt internationally, but nothing compared to

Crowds gather in celebration of equality, first at the Lincoln Memorial, along the Reflecting Pool, and then at the Washington Monument.

the outcome it had on the black community. Aaron Henry, then Mississippi's NAACP president, was quoted in Time-Life's *I Have a Dream: The Story of Martin Luther King in Text and Pictures* as saying, "There has been a re-evaluation of our slave philosophy that permitted us to be satisfied with the leftovers at the back door rather than demand a full serving at the family dinner table."

THE RIPPLE EFFECT

Dr. King used his masterful public speaking talents to tie together concepts from the Bible, the Emancipation Proclamation, Negro spirituals, and patriotic songs. By doing so, he appealed to people from all walks of life. Brian Ward, professor of American studies at Northumbria University, made this observation, according to Claire Bates of BBC.co.uk: "[Dr. King] was portraying himself as a quintessentially American leader pursuing American goals, and this appealed to northern liberals. Civil rights were now seen to be in keeping with the ideals of Middle America." But the day's events also showed one thing: it took a unified force to dream Dr. King's dream. The same article notes Zoe Colley's thoughts as a Dundee University lecturer on civil rights history: "We shouldn't forget beneath [Dr. King] there were thousands of people in the civil rights movement plugging away in a patchwork of communities across towns and cities."

"A LOVE THAT FORGIVES"

Not everyone was touched by the events of the March on Washington. Demonstrators in Alabama waved

INNOCENCE LOST

The bombing of the 16th Street Baptist Church affected many, one of whom was Condoleezza Rice, former U.S. secretary of state. She was a child at the time, but as other American children were playing and exploring during their youth, she was confined to her neighborhood, living in fear that racism would come knocking on her door.

Rice recalled what it was like growing up in Birmingham. "There was no sanctuary," she told Verna Gates of Reuters.com. "There was no place really safe." This was especially true with the 16th Street Baptist Church bombing. Rice had lost a playmate, Denise McNair. She recounted, "Everyone in the black community knew one of those girls." The girls were known for their strong suits: Addie Mae Collins was an artist; Carole Robertson, a straight-A student; Cynthia Wesley, a math whiz; and McNair, an entertainer who raised money for charity. Today, Rice cherishes a photo of McNair, who is pictured accepting a school certificate from Rice's father, a pastor in the community.

But it was not only a friend that Rice lost that day; she also lost her youthful innocence. Her father attempted to console her, but the impression had been forever sealed in her mind. In looking back, Rice understood the disaster revealed our humanity, and it was this realization that would eventually unite the community. She later took this lesson to the White House. As Secretary of State, Rice empathized with victims of terrorist attacks, especially with those from Palestine and Israel. "I told them I know what it is like for a Palestinian mother, who has to tell her child they can't go somewhere," Rice said in a Reuters.com article, "and how it is for an Israeli mother, who puts her child to bed and wonders if the child will be alive in the morning."

antidesegregation posters and Confederate flags at public schools. The Birmingham Board of Education closed three public schools. Firebombs were set off. But nothing compared to what was to come.

It was a quiet Sunday morning at the 16th Street Baptist Church on September 15, 1963. "A Love That Forgives" was the day's lesson. As the young girls eagerly prepared in the basement lounge, a dynamite blast resonated throughout

Pictured here are the four young girls who died at the 16th Street Baptist Church *(clockwise from top left)*: Denise McNair, Carole Robertson, Addie Mae Collins, and Cynthia Wesley.

the church. Twenty-three people were injured. In the debris, the bodies of the four girls were found: eleven-year-old Denise McNair and fourteen-year-olds Addie Mae Collins, Carole Robertson, and Cynthia Wesley. Law enforcement determined that the dynamite had been hidden beneath the stairs. Several KKK members were arrested, but they were only charged with dynamite possession. Robertson's funeral was on September 17, and the funeral for the other three girls was held at the 16th Street Baptist Church the following day. Here, King delivered a heartfelt eulogy before thousands of mourners. According to *A Call to Conscience*, he declared the girls to be "martyred heroines of a holy crusade for freedom and human dignity."

Chapter 5

THE LEGACY REMEMBERED

With President Kennedy's assassination in Dallas, Texas, on November 22, 1963, Vice President Lyndon B. Johnson (1908–1973) took up the civil rights legislation immediately. Despite strong opposition, he signed the Civil Rights Act of 1964 into law on July 2. Among the many public figures in attendance were Martin Luther King Jr. and Rosa Parks. However, the new legislation was not a complete victory. Short term, voters were restricted to a standard of sixth-grade-level literacy. Long term, violent discrimination still rocked the South.

AND THEN THERE WAS SELMA

In 1965, Dr. King, the SCLC, and SNCC targeted Selma, Alabama, for black voter registration in the South. Nearly half of Selma's population was African American, but 99 percent of the voters were white. The sheriff, James Clark (1922–2007), was a segregationist with Ku Klux Klan deputies. Each time African Americans came to the registrar, Clark turned them away or arrested them on trumped-up charges. If they

KING ACCEPTS THE NOBEL PEACE PRIZE

Although he invented dynamite, Swedish chemist Alfred Nobel (1833–1896) was a pacifist intrigued by the peace movement. When his brother died in 1888, a French newspaper made a severe error and printed an obituary for Alfred. The obituary stated Alfred was the "merchant of death." To rectify his legacy, Nobel left a will offering five annual prizes to those who have made significant strides for the benefit of humanity. Since 1901, Nobel Prizes have honored individuals in the fields of chemistry, literature, physics, physiology or medicine, and peace. A five-person committee—chosen by the Norwegian parliament—selects the winner, and the prize is awarded in Oslo, Norway.

Pride among the black community swelled when it learned that Martin Luther King Jr. would receive the prestigious Nobel Peace Prize on December 10, 1964. At age thirty-five, he would be the youngest winner. And yet, Dr. King was perplexed as to why such an award would be given when the end result—peace—had not yet been established. The Nobel Peace Prize Committee did not offer a reason. According to Time-Life's *I Have a Dream*, Dr. King stated the following during his acceptance speech:

After contemplation, I conclude that this award which I receive on behalf of that movement is profound recognition that nonviolence is the answer to the crucial political and moral question of our time—the need for man to overcome oppression and violence without resorting to violence and oppression.

Dr. King also accepted the cash prize of $54,000 and donated it all to the civil rights movement.

did make it to voter registrars, they were required to fill out complicated applications and complete intense literacy tests. The march would put national pressure on the Johnson administration to enact new voting rights legislation. Four hundred marchers participated that February evening, but they were met by attacking Alabama state troopers and local police. Amid the hubbub, Jimmie Lee Jackson (1938–1965) was shot while protecting his mother from a nightstick beating. Ignoring Governor Wallace's order forbidding demonstrations, Dr. King called for a 50-mile (80-km) march from Selma to Alabama's capital, Montgomery. He was in Atlanta at the time, but his colleagues led the march. Demonstrators made their way through Selma but were confronted by sixty state troopers and deputies who were waiting at the Edmund Pettus Bridge. When they refused to retreat, the law officials attacked with clubs and tear gas. Mounted police trampled on those who had fallen to the ground. By the end of the day, seventy-eight African Americans were hospitalized. What was called "Bloody Sunday" outraged the nation. Riots broke out in the streets of U.S. and Canadian cities. The black

Protesters of all ages take to the streets in a civil rights march from Selma to Montgomery, Alabama, in 1965.

community responded with "We Shall Overcome," and Dr. King called for another march.

President Johnson addressed the nation, detailing the Voting Rights Act that he planned to submit to Congress. He even used the slogan "We Shall Overcome" in his speech. Although Dr. King called for a second Selma-to-Montgomery

King and other civil rights leaders stand in support as President Lyndon B. Johnson signs the Voting Rights Act in the Capitol Rotunda in 1965.

march, it was canceled at the request of federal officials who feared another bloody confrontation. A third march was planned but delayed in time for a federal judge to hand down an injunction preventing Wallace from obstructing the march and ordering him to protect the marchers. Wallace pleaded "lack of funds," so President Johnson sent in federal troops to protect the protesters. This third attempt was successful, as demonstrators walked around the clock for three days, eventually reaching Montgomery. Dr. King led the march. He was also present when Johnson signed the Voting Rights Act into law in 1965. Dr. King was given one of the signing pens.

THE ASSASSINATION OF DR. KING

Now that the Voting Rights Act was law, Dr. King focused on socioeconomic issues, such as poverty and unemployment. In 1966, he moved his family into an apartment in Chicago's black ghetto. He then started a campaign to end housing, employment, and school discrimination. He led marches, was imprisoned, ran additional campaigns, and facilitated strikes. He spoke out on America's involvement in the Vietnam War, despite criticism from many across the nation. Dr. King was viewed as unpatriotic, but that didn't stop him from forging ahead for equality on the home front.

April 4, 1968, had started off as a joyous day. Dr. King and his advisers were sharing a relaxing Thursday, telling jokes and heading for dinner out. As the afternoon rolled into evening, he stood on the second-floor balcony of the Lorraine Motel in Memphis, Tennessee. A shot pierced him in the neck. Although Dr. King was rushed to the hospital, it was too late—the civil rights leader was pronounced dead. Escaped convict and known racist James Earl Ray would later be convicted for the murder.

The news of Dr. King's assassination resounded around the world. Riots broke out in more than one hundred U.S. cities; $45 million worth of property was destroyed. Twenty-seven thousand people were arrested, and forty-six people died. Many believed the assassination was a rejection of their passionate yet nonviolent pursuit of equality, and Dr. King's death seemed to broaden the gap between black

LET HIS
DEATH
NOT BE IN
VAIN

After King's 1968 assassination, public reaction varied from nonviolent vigils to acts of violence. In this photograph, demonstrators make a statement in front of the White House.

and white Americans. President Johnson addressed a mourning nation as noted on PBS.org:

> Once again, the heart of America is heavy—the spirit of America is heavy—the spirit of America weeps—for a tragedy that denies the very meaning of our land. The life of a man who symbolized the freedom and faith of America has been taken. But it is the fiber and the fabric of the Republic that is being tested. If we are to have the America that we mean to have, all men—of all races, all regions, all religions—must stand their ground to deny violence its victory in this sorrowful time and in all times to come.

Johnson declared a national day of mourning on Sunday, April 7. He also implored Congress to accelerate the passing of additional civil rights legislation. It responded, and on April 11, Johnson signed the Civil Rights Act of 1968—also known as the Fair Housing Act—into law.

THE MOVEMENT CONTINUED

In the weeks after her husband's funeral, Coretta Scott King picked up where Dr. King left off. She had stood by his side all those years and pressed on for racial and economic justice. Mrs. King also connected with world leaders and advocated for world issues, such as education, environmental justice, gay and lesbian rights, health care, nuclear disarmament, and the rights of women and children. In 1968, Mrs. King founded the Atlanta-based Martin Luther King Jr. Center for Nonviolent Social Change (The King Center).

A MAN REMEMBERED, A DREAM IMMORTALIZED

August 28, 2013, marked the fiftieth anniversary of the March on Washington. The nation celebrated by turning its eyes once again to the National Mall in Washington, D.C. It is where the Martin Luther King Jr. Memorial now stands. People from around the world joined in the celebration to witness President Barack Obama, political leaders, entertainers, and members of the King family raise their voices in honor of the man who called upon his faith, talents, fortitude, and countrymen to realize equality for all.

Dr. King will be remembered forever as a leader among leaders, a man who overcame fear and championed for the rights of every man, woman, and child. Despite adversity, he revived the world with these words from his final speech, "I've Been to the Mountaintop." It was delivered at Mason Temple Church in Memphis, Tennessee, on April 3, 1968:

> Well, I don't know what will happen now. We've got some difficult days ahead. But it doesn't matter with me now. Because I've been to the mountaintop. And I don't mind. Like anybody, I would like to live a long life. Longevity has its place. But I'm not concerned about that now. I just want to do God's will. And He's allowed me to go up to the mountain. And I've looked over. And I've seen the Promised Land. I may not get there with you. But I want you to know tonight, that we, as a people will get to the Promised Land. And I'm happy, tonight. I'm not

"I Have A Dream" is etched on the steps of the Lincoln Memorial. It encourages a nation, and the world, to champion for "equality for all."

worried about anything. I'm not fearing any man. Mine eyes have seen the glory of the coming of the Lord! (As quoted in *Martin Luther King's Biblical Epic: His Final Great Speech.*)

Martin Luther King Jr.—husband, father, minister, activist, and Nobel Peace Prize winner who fought for our freedom. He was a trailblazer, a hero, and the ultimate kind of dreamer.

I ask you today, "What is your dream?"

January 15, 1929 Michael King (Martin Luther King Jr.) is born in Atlanta, Georgia.

1954 *Brown v. Board of Education* outlaws segregation in schools. The U.S. Supreme Court orders schools to desegregate.

December 1, 1955 Rosa Parks refuses to give up her bus seat, which ignites the Montgomery bus boycott in Montgomery, Alabama.

September 1957 President Eisenhower sends federal troops to ensure the entry of the Little Rock Nine.

September 9, 1957 Congress passes the Civil Rights Act of 1957.

May 1961 Freedom Riders leave Washington, D.C., and head for Anniston, Alabama, where segregationists were waiting.

April 1963 The Birmingham Campaign begins. Dr. King and Ralph Abernathy are arrested for demonstrating without a permit. Dr. King pens his "Letter from Birmingham Jail."

May 1963 The Children's Crusade takes place in Birmingham, Alabama.

June 11, 1963 Governor Wallace stands in the door, refusing to allow the entry of African American students into the University of Alabama.

August 28, 1963 Dr. King leads the March on Washington for Jobs and Freedom and delivers his famous "I Have a Dream" speech.

September 15, 1963 A dynamite blast kills four African American girls at the 16th Street Baptist Church in Birmingham, Alabama.

July 2, 1964 Dr. King attends the signing ceremony of the Civil Rights Act of 1964 at the White House.

December 10, 1964 Dr. King is awarded the Nobel Peace Prize in Oslo, Norway.

March 1965 Dr. King calls for a 50-mile (80-km) march from Selma, Alabama, to Montgomery, Alabama, in the name of voting rights.

August 6, 1965 The Voting Rights Act is signed into law by President Johnson.

April 3, 1968 Dr. King delivers his last speech, "I've Been to the Mountaintop," at a Mason Temple rally in Memphis, Tennessee.

April 4, 1968 Dr. King is shot and killed in Memphis, Tennessee.

GLOSSARY

AGAPE Love that is extended to all.

BOYCOTT A coordinated effort designed to avoid the purchase of products and services from a particular person or company.

CAMPAIGN An organized social or political work designed to solicit a particular goal or render a specific outcome.

CIVIL DISOBEDIENCE A peaceful protest against a form of perceived injustice.

CIVIL RIGHTS The enforceable rights or privileges of individuals to receive fair political and social treatment.

COURT INJUNCTION A court order requiring a person to perform an act or restraining someone from committing an act.

DISCRIMINATION The act of treating a person or group differently based on race, age, gender, nationality, sexual orientation, marital status, disability, or religion.

EMANCIPATION The act or process of being set free from any legal, political, or social restrictions.

FIRST-CLASS CITIZEN The highest class of citizen who enjoys a full range of socioeconomic opportunities, as well as civil and legal rights.

INTEGRATION The act of bringing people together from various demographics, especially racial groups.

LITERACY TEST A reading test required by law that if passed, allows a person to vote.

LYNCHING The illegal act of a disorderly group of people who murders a person thought to be guilty of unproven deeds.

RUNOFF ELECTION A "round two" election in which the two top candidates from the previous too-close-to-call election run again.

SECOND-CLASS CITIZEN A person who is routinely discriminated against within a political jurisdiction despite his or her citizenship status.

SEGREGATION The act of separating a person or group from the majority.

SHARECROPPER A tenant farmer who raises crops and uses a portion of the harvest to pay rent.

SIT-IN A nonviolent act in which protesters refuse to leave an often prohibited location until their demands are met.

THEOLOGY The study of religion.

Boston University School of Theology
745 Commonwealth Avenue
Boston, MA 02215
(617) 353-3050
Website: http://www.bu.edu/sth
The School of Theology was the founding school of today's
    Boston University. It is the oldest United Methodist semi-
    nary in North America.

Canadian Civil Liberties Association (CCLA)
215 Spadina Avenue, Suite 210
Toronto, ON M5T 2C7
Canada
(416) 363-0321
Website: http://ccla.org
Since 1964, the Canadian Civil Liberties Association has pro-
    moted and defended respect for human rights and civil
    liberties.

Canadian Human Rights Commission (CHRC)
344 Slater Street, 8th Floor
Ottawa, ON K1A 1E1
Canada
(888) 214-1090
Website: http://www.chrc-ccdp.ca/eng
Established in 1977 by the Canadian government, the
    CHRC ensures equal employment opportunities for
    every Canadian. It also helps protect those confronted by
    discrimination according to the Canadian Human Rights
    Act and the Employment Equity Act.

Congress of Racial Equality (CORE)
P.O. Box 264 Cooper Station
New York, NY 10276
(212) 598-4000
Website: http://www.core-online.org
Founded by an interracial group of Chicago-based students
    in 1942, CORE worked with Dr. King in promoting non-
    violence during the American civil rights movement.

Crozer Theological Seminary
42 Upland Avenue
Brookhaven, PA 19015
The Crozer Theological Seminary was an American Baptist
    Church school that trained theological students for work
    in the Baptist ministry.

Martin Luther King Jr. Center for Nonviolent Social Change
449 Auburn Avenue NE
Atlanta, GA 30312
(404) 526-8900
Website: http://www.thekingcenter.org
Also known as the King Center, this organization celebrates the
    life and work of Martin Luther King Jr.

Morehouse College
830 Westview Drive SW
Atlanta, GA 30314
(404) 681-2800
Website: http://www.morehouse.edu
Founded in 1867, Morehouse College has been a private, all-
    male, liberal arts college in Atlanta, Georgia.

National Association for the Advancement of Colored
People (NAACP)
4805 Mount Hope Drive
Baltimore, MD 21215
(877) NAACP-98
Website: http://www.naacp.org
Known as the oldest civil rights organization in the United
States, the NAACP has worked to safeguard equality and
eliminate discrimination for all Americans.

Southern Christian Leadership Conference (SCLC)
320 Auburn Avenue NE
Atlanta, GA 30303
(404) 522-1420
Website: http://www.sclcnational.org
Founded in January 10, 1957, the SCLC promotes spiritual
principles within the community while advocating for
personal responsibility, leadership, and community service.
It endorses affirmative action and works for justice against
discrimination.

WEBSITES

Due to the changing nature of Internet links, Rosen Publishing
has developed an online list of websites related to the subject
of this book. This site is updated regularly. Please use this link
to access the list:

http://www.rosenlinks.com/CCRM/MLK

FOR FURTHER READING

Arsenault, Raymond. *Freedom Riders: 1961 and the Struggle for Racial Justice.* New York, NY: Oxford University Press, 2011.

Bagley, Edythe Scott. *Desert Rose: The Life and Legacy of Coretta Scott King.* Tuscaloosa, AL: University of Alabama Press, 2012.

Bowers, Rick. *Spies of Mississippi: The True Story of the Spy Network That Tried to Destroy the Civil Rights Movement.* Washington, DC: National Geographic Society, 2010.

Brimner, Larry Dane. *Black & White: The Confrontation Between Reverend Fred L. Shuttlesworth and Eugene "Bull" Connor.* Honesdale, PA: Calkins Creek, 2011.

Easwaran, Eknath. *Gandhi the Man: How One Man Changed Himself to Change the World.* Tomales, CA: Blue Mountain Center of Meditation, 2011.

Jones, William P. *The March on Washington: Jobs, Freedom, and the Forgotten History of Civil Rights.* New York, NY: W. W. Norton and Co., 2013.

Kelley, Kitty. *Let Freedom Ring: Stanley Tretick's Iconic Images of the March on Washington.* New York, NY: Thomas Dune Books, 2013.

King, Martin Luther, Jr. *Strength to Love.* Minneapolis, MN: Fortress Press, 2010.

King, Martin Luther, Jr. *Stride for Freedom.* Boston, MA: Beacon Press, 2010.

King, Martin Luther, Jr. *A Time to Break Silence: The Essential Works of Martin Luther King Jr. for Students.* Boston, MA: Beacon Press, 2013.

Lanier, Carlotta Walls, and Lisa Frazier Page. *A Mighty Long Way: My Journey to Justice at Little Rock Central High School.* New York, NY: Oneworld Books, 2009.

Levinson, Cynthia. *We've Got a Job: The 1963 Birmingham Children's March*. Atlanta, GA: Peachtree Publishers, 2012.

May, Gary. *Bending Toward Justice: The Voting Rights Act and the Transformation of American Democracy*. New York, NY: Basic Books, 2013.

Nathan, Amy. *Round and Round Together: Taking a Merry-Go-Round Ride into the Civil Rights Movement*. Philadelphia, PA: Paul Dry Books, 2011.

Phibbs, Cheryl. *The Montgomery Bus Boycott: A History and Reference Guide*. Santa Barbara, CA: ABC-CLIO, 2009.

Posner, Gerald. *Killing the Dream: James Earl Ray and the Assassination of Martin Luther King Jr.* New York, NY: Open Road Integrated Media, 2013.

Taylor, Anthony. *The Life-Changing Lessons and Story of Martin Luther King: The Fight for a Dream*. Seattle, WA: Amazon Digital Services, 2013.

Thoreau, Henry David. *Civil Disobedience*. Philadelphia, PA: Empire Books, 2013.

Tougas, Shelley. *Little Rock Girl 1957: How a Photograph Changed the Fight for Integration*. Minneapolis, MN: CompassPoint Books, 2011.

Younge, Gary. *The Speech: The Story Behind Dr. Martin Luther King Jr.'s Dream*. Chicago, IL: Haymarket Books, 2013.

Adair, Lolita Kelsey. Interview with the author. November 2, 2013.

Bates, Claire. "Martin Luther King's 'I Have a Dream' Speech: What Does It Tell Us About Him?" Bbc.co.uk, 2013. Retrieved December 1, 2013 (http://www.bbc.co.uk/history/0/23815398).

Bates, Daisy. *The Long Shadow of Little Rock: A Memoir.* Fayetteville, AK: University of Arkansas Press, 1989.

Bell, Debra. "George Wallace Stood in a Doorway at the University of Alabama 50 Years Ago Today." *US News & World Report,* June 11 2013. Retrieved November 3, 2013 (http://www.usnews.com/news/blogs/press-past/2013/06/11/george-wallace-stood-in-a-doorway-at-the-university-of-alabama-50-years-ago-today).

Biography.com. "Rosa Parks." 2013. Retrieved July 30, 2013 (http://www.biography.com/people/rosa-parks-9433715?page=1).

Carson, Clayborne. *The Autobiography of Martin Luther King Jr.* New York, NY: The Heirs to the Estate of Martin Luther King Jr., 1998.

Carson, Clayborne, Kris Shepard, and Andrew Young. *A Call to Conscience: The Landmark Speeches of Dr. Martin Luther King Jr.* New York, NY: The Heirs to the Estate of Martin Luther King Jr., 2001.

CRF-USA.org. "The Civil Rights Acts of 1964." Retrieved July 4, 2013 (http://www.crf-usa.org/black-history-month/the-civil-rights-act-of-1964).

Gates, Verna. "Condoleezza Rice Recalls Racial Blast That Killed Childhood Friend." Reuters.com, September 14, 2013. Retrieved November 30, 2013

(http://www.reuters.com/article/2013/09/14/
us-usa-alabama-memorial-idUSBRE98C11720130914).

Gross, Terry. "Get on the Bus: The Freedom Riders of
1961." NPR.org, January 12, 2006. Retrieved October
3, 2013 (http://www.npr.org/2006/01/12/5149667/
get-on-the-bus-the-freedom-riders-of-1961).

History.com "Black Codes." Retrieved August 7, 2013
(http://www.history.com/topics/black-codes).

Joiner, Lottie L. "How the Children of Birmingham Changed
the Civil-Rights Movement." TheDailyBeast.com,
2013. Retrieved June 19, 2013 (http://www.thedailybeast
.com/articles/2013/05/02/how-the-children-of-birming-
ham-changed-the-civil-rights-movement.html).

King, Martin Luther, Jr. "I Have A Dream…" National
Archives, 1963. Retrieved December 1, 2013 (http://
www.archives.gov).

King, Martin Luther, Jr. *The Papers of Martin Luther King
Jr.: Volume III: Birth of a New Age, December 1955–
December 1956.* Berkeley, CA: University of California
Press, 1997.

King Institute. "Martin Luther King Jr. and the Global
Freedom Struggle." Retrieved August 7, 2013 (http://
mlk-kpp01.stanford.edu/index.php/encyclopedia/
documentsentry/doc_460806_000).

McCain, John, and Mark Salter. *Character Is Destiny:
Inspiring Stories Every Young Person Should Know and
Every Adult Should Remember.* New York, NY: Random
House, 2005.

Mieder, Wolfgang. *"Making a Way Out of No Way": Martin
Luther King's Sermonic Proverbial Rhetoric.* New York, NY:
Peter Lang Publishing, 2010.

Miller, Keith D. *Martin Luther King's Biblical Epic: His Final, Great Speech.* New York, NY: University Press of Mississippi, 2012.

Mohn, Tanya. "Martin Luther King Jr.: The German Connection and How He Got His Name." Forbes.com, January 12, 2012. Retrieved August 6, 2013 (http:// www.forbes.com/sites/tanyamohn/2012/01/12/ martin-luther-king-jr-the-german-connection-and -how-he-got-his-name).

Osborne, Charles, ed. *I Have a Dream: The Story of Martin Luther King in Text and Pictures.* New York, NY: Time, 1968.

PBS.org. "Address to the Nation Upon Proclaiming a Day of Mourning." 1968. Retrieved July 4, 2013 (http:// www.pbs.org/wgbh/americanexperience/features/ primary-resources/lbj-mourning).

INDEX

ABOUT THE AUTHOR

From age two, Erin Staley has had dance shoes on her feet. She continued her love for the performance arts as a student at Bowling Green State University. One summer, she jumped at the chance of traveling to Ghana, West Africa. She immersed herself in the culture and walked in the steps of Martin Luther King Jr. He had traveled there nearly forty years prior, but his optimism and faith had left its mark. For the next two decades, Staley shared the joy of movement and the dream of brotherhood with people of all ages, races, religions, and creeds. Now working as a writer in Mexico, she continues to reach out to audiences all over the world to promote unity.

PHOTO CREDITS

Cover, p. 21 Hulton Archive/Archive Photos/Getty Images; pp. 4, 56–57, 60–61 Library of Congress Prints and Photographs Division; p. 8 Robert W. Kelley/Time & Life Pictures/Getty Images; pp. 11, 12–13, 35, 52 © AP Images; pp. 14–15, 31 Underwood Archives/Archive Photos/Getty Images; pp. 26–27, 46–47 Francis Miller/Time & Life Pictures/Getty Images; p. 28 Frank Scherschel/Time & Life Pictures/ Getty Images; pp. 36–37 Michael Ochs Archives/Getty images; p. 39 Ernst Haas/Getty Images; p. 44 Leonard McCombe/Time & Life Pictures/Getty Images; p. 49 Bob Parent/Hulton Archive/Getty Images; pp. 58–59 LBJ Library photo by Yoichi Okamoto; p. 64 Richard Cavalleri/Shutterstock.com; cover and interior background images © iStockphoto.com/Victor Pelaez (U.S. Constitution facsimile), © iStockphoto.com/klikk (American flag).

Designer: Nicole Russo; Editor: Heather Moore Niver; Photo Researcher: Nicole DiMella